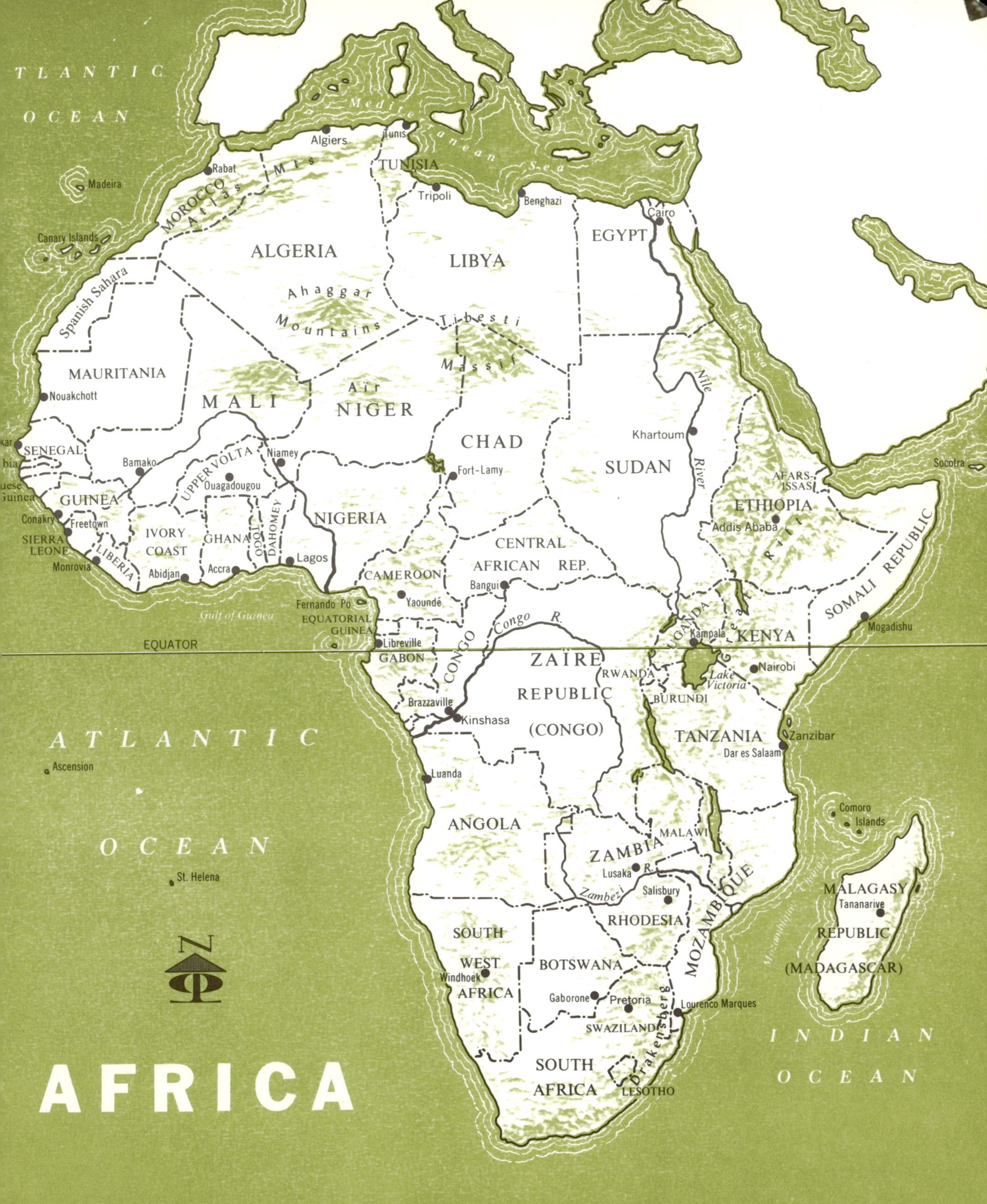

TLANTIC
OCEAN
Madeira
Canary Islands
Spanish Sahara
MAURITANIA
Nouakchott
Rabat
MOROCCO
Atlas Mts
Algiers
Tunis
TUNISIA
Tripoli
Benghazi
ALGERIA
LIBYA
Mediterranean Sea
EGYPT
Cairo
Ahaggar Mountains
Tibesti Massif
Aïr
MALI
NIGER
CHAD
Nile River
Khartoum
SUDAN
Red Sea
Socotra
AFARS-ISSAS
ETHIOPIA
Addis Ababa
SENEGAL
kar
bia
uese
Guinea
GUINEA
Conakry
Freetown
SIERRA LEONE
Monrovia
LIBERIA
Bamako
UPPER VOLTA
Ouagadougou
Niamey
IVORY COAST
GHANA
TOGO
DAHOMEY
NIGERIA
Lagos
Accra
Abidjan
CAMEROON
Fort-Lamy
CENTRAL AFRICAN REP.
Bangui
Great Rift Valley
SOMALI REPUBLIC
Mogadishu
Fernando Po
Gulf of Guinea
EQUATORIAL GUINEA
Libreville
GABON
Yaoundé
EQUATOR
Congo
Congo R.
ZAÏRE REPUBLIC
(CONGO)
UGANDA
Kampala
KENYA
Lake Victoria
Nairobi
RWANDA
BURUNDI
ATLANTIC
Ascension
OCEAN
Brazzaville
Kinshasa
TANZANIA
Dar es Salaam
Zanzibar
Luanda
ANGOLA
ZAMBIA
Lusaka
MALAWI
Zambezi R.
Mozambique Channel
Comoro Islands
St. Helena
SOUTH WEST AFRICA
Windhoek
BOTSWANA
RHODESIA
Salisbury
MOZAMBIQUE
MALAGASY
Tananarive
REPUBLIC
(MADAGASCAR)
Gaborone
Pretoria
Drakensberg
Lourenço Marques
SWAZILAND
SOUTH AFRICA
LESOTHO
INDIAN OCEAN
N
AFRICA

RWANDA

by **ALLAN CARPENTER**
and **MATTHEW MAGINNIS**

Consulting Editor
Ethel M. Albert
Department of Anthropology
Northwestern University
Evanston, Illinois

CHILDRENS PRESS, CHICAGO

THE ENCHANTMENT OF AFRICA

Available now: Botswana, Burundi, Egypt, Kenya, Malagasy Republic (Madagascar), Rwanda, Tunisia, Uganda, Zambia
Planned for the future (six each season): Algeria, Cameroon, Central African Republic, Chad, Congo (Brazzaville), Dahomey, Equatorial Guinea, Ethiopia, Gambia, Gabon, Ghana, Guinea, Ivory Coast, Lesotho, Liberia, Libya, Malawi, Mali, Mauritania, Morocco, Niger, Nigeria, Rhodesia, Senegal, Sierra Leone, Somali Republic, South Africa, Sudan, Swaziland, Tanzania, Togo, Upper Volta, Zaïre Republic (Congo Kinshasha)

ACKNOWLEDGMENTS

E. Michael Southwick, Vice Consul, Embassy of the United States of America, Kigali, Rwanda; Embassy of Rwanda, Washington, D.C.; Chris C. Pollet, Counselor of Tourism, Kigali, Rwanda; Permanent Mission of Rwanda to the United Nations, New York; Melville J. Herskovits Library of African Studies, Northwestern University, Evanston, Illinois

Cover Photograph: Children at a schoolyard, Allan Carpenter
Frontispiece: Musicians, Ministry of Information, Zaïre Republic

Series Coordinator: Michael Roberts
Project Editor: Joan Downing
Assistant Editor: Janis Fortman
Manuscript Editor: Elizabeth Rhein
Map Artist: Donald G. Bouma

j 916.75 71
C

LIBRARY OF CONGRESS CATALOGING IN PUBLICATION DATA

Carpenter, John Allan, 1917—
    Rwanda.
    (Enchantment of Africa)

    SUMMARY: Introduces the geography, history, government, industries, culture, and people of the small country, located in the mountains of east-central Africa, which gained independence in 1962.

    I. Rwanda—Juvenile literature. (1. Rwanda)
I. Maginnis, Matthew, joint author. II. Title.
DT449.R9C3   916.7'571   73-4972
ISBN 0-516-04581-4

Contents

MINISTRY OF INFORMATION, KAMPALA, UGANDA

A Folktale to Set the Scene

For generations children in Rwanda have listened to folktales told by their elders. This is one of their favorites.

HOW DOG CAME TO LIVE WITH MAN

Long ago Dog and Leopard were friends. Some people say these two animals were always enemies, but those people do not know the real story.

When Dog and Leopard were friends, they lived together in a cave. For a long time, Dog and Leopard got along well. They took turns hunting for food and shared whatever they killed. Of course, Leopard was the better hunter because he was bigger and stronger. Dog began to get fat from eating all the meat Leopard hunted.

As time went on, Dog became fatter and lazier. Finally he was not doing any of the hard work of hunting. Instead, when he went off into the woods to hunt, he would find a nice, flat rock warmed by the sun, where he would soon fall asleep. Later, he would tell Leopard about a lovely, fat bird he had almost caught. After a while, Dog realized that his stories had become tiresome. Leopard thought Dog should have something more to show for his trips to the woods, so Dog thought of a way to bring home meat without working for it.

Dog and Leopard were friends until Dog became lazy and tried to trick Leopard.

One day Leopard said, "I have seen a fat, black-and-white goat tied near the houses on the hill. Tonight I am going to steal it."

"Really?" answered Dog. "I have been watching a black-and-white goat, too. I thought I would go hunting tonight."

That night Dog and Leopard started off toward the houses on the hill. At the edge of the woods, they separated. Quietly, Dog hid where he could watch his friend.

Leopard crept toward the houses. In seconds he had killed the goat. Right away Dog began to make a lot of noise. Disguising his voice, he shouted, "Quick! Get your spears! Leopard has stolen a goat!"

Leopard was frightened. He dropped the goat and ran. Quickly, Dog grabbed the goat and dragged it home. "Look what I have brought!" he called to Leopard. "Did you have good luck?"

Leopard told him how he had been discovered and chased away. Dog invited Leopard to share his goat.

A few nights later, Leopard went to raid another goat pen. Dog tricked him in the same way. This time, when Dog had dragged the goat almost back to the cave, where Leopard could easily hear him, he tried still another trick. Using the same voice as before, he shouted, "There he is!

Kill him! That dog stole our goat! Kill him!" As loud as he could, he beat the dead goat with a stick.

When Leopard heard all this, he thought Dog had been tracked by the farmer. He ran away into the forest, and Dog ate the goat himself. When Leopard returned, Dog told him of his narrow escape from his pursuers.

Dog continued to trick Leopard in this way for a long time. Leopard did not suspect his friend since he was worried about his own bad luck. He decided to seek advice from Rabbit, who was very clever.

Rabbit listened and said, "Beware of Dog." Then he ran away.

That night, Dog and Leopard went to steal an animal from a farm far away. As usual they separated, and as soon as Leopard had killed his prey, the shouting started. This time Leopard did not run away; he went toward the voice—and found Dog.

Around the animal pen and through the garden, Dog ran for his life. He ran right into the house of Man. Startled, Man leaped out of bed and grabbed his spear, but dog wagged his tail and showed himself to be so friendly that Man did not kill him. Since that day, Man and Dog have been friends.

The Face of the Land

Rwanda lies tucked away high in the mountains of east-central Africa. It is one of the smallest in size among all of the countries on the African continent. With an area of 10,169 square miles, Rwanda is about the size of the state of Maryland.

Rwanda is completely landlocked. It is tucked in between four neighbors: Uganda to the north; Tanzania to the east; Burundi to the south; and Zaïre (formerly called the Belgian Congo and then the Democratic Republic of the Congo) to the

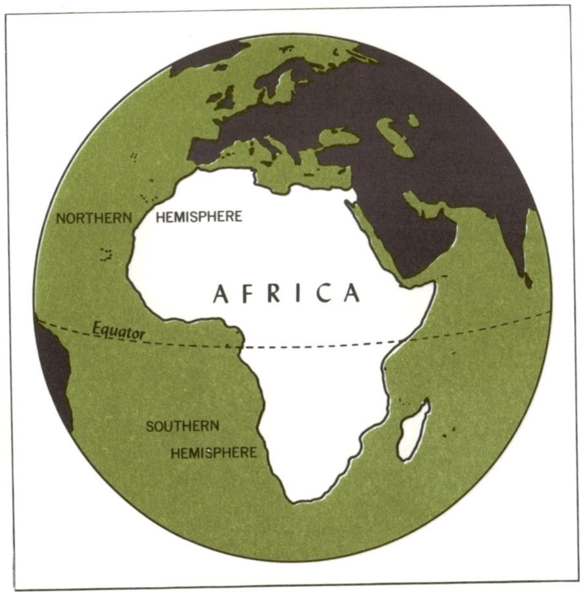

west. The nearest seacoast, which touches on the Indian Ocean, is seven hundred miles to the east in Kenya. To the west, the Atlantic Ocean is twice as far away.

Rwanda lies in the heart of the lake region of Africa in an area often called "High Africa." The country has a highly irregular shape. Long stretches of its borders are formed by rivers, mountains, and lakes.

CONGO-NILE DIVIDING CREST

The dominant feature of Rwanda's geography is a line of mountains running north to south through the western part of the country. These mountains are the Congo-Nile dividing crest. Their peaks divide the watersheds of Africa's two greatest rivers, the Nile and the Congo. Rain that falls on one side of the mountains runs down into the Nile River; rain falling on the other side runs into the Congo River.

A spectacular natural phenomenon, this mountain rise in remote Rwanda is like two giant sliding boards that are set back to back. Down each side the waters gush through short, unnavigable rivers on a fantastic journey.

On the east these rivers head for the Nile, the river that keeps Egypt alive. Waters from this river made possible the great civilization of the pharaohs. Eventually, water from the Nile flows into the Mediterranean Sea.

On the west the mountains send water into the three-thousand-mile-long system of the Congo River. These waters travel across the continent, joining waters from dozens of tributaries; they travel over mountains, savannas, rapids, and rain forests before reaching the Atlantic Ocean.

Until 1877 no one was sure where this fantastic water network began or ended. In that year, Henry Morton Stanley solved the mystery of the Congo River.

Stanley had already proved himself as an adventurer through many accomplishments, such as locating the famous Scottish missionary-explorer, Dr. David Livingstone, in eastern Africa. His calm greeting—"Dr. Livingstone, I presume?"—to the man for whom he had dared great dangers made him famous, too. Partly to carry on the work of Livingstone, Stanley set out to do an incredibly difficult thing: to trace the course of the Congo River. Starting in the east, where the sources of the Congo rise, he followed the river west all the way to the Atlantic.

The majority of his party of three hundred, almost all of them Africans, died of

Rwanda is sometimes called "the land of lakes, rivers, and mountains." In the background are terraced slopes where farmers cultivate their crops.

disease on the way. Their brave expedition is one of history's greatest voyages of exploration.

THE GREAT RIFT VALLEY

The peaks of the Congo-Nile dividing crest average about nine thousand feet above sea level, some of them reaching almost ten thousand feet.

These mountains form the rim of Africa's Rift Valley, part of which passes through Rwanda. A *rift* is a separation, or breaking apart. The Rift Valley is actually a chain of valleys, canyons, lakes, and seas running from the Middle East to south-central Africa. Its formation began millions of years ago, when the earth's crust started to crack under pressure from deep below the surface. In some places great pieces of the earth's surface caved in; in other places huge masses of soil and rock were pushed and piled by the swelling and cracking from within.

As the centuries passed, the eruption of volcanoes and the effects of erosion changed the face of the land even more. Some of the new valleys filled with water. The Red Sea, which is the eastern border of Egypt, was formed in this way; so was Lake Kivu, on the northwestern border of Rwanda.

The rift itself extends all the way from Jordan in the Middle East to Mozambique in southeast Africa and out into the Indian Ocean. In some places it is more than fifty miles wide, and the gradual process of pressure, cracking, and collapse may continue indefinitely.

The part of Rwanda west of the Congo-Nile dividing crest, between the mountains and Lake Kivu, is the Rift Valley. There are some rich volcanic soils in this

MAP KEY

Akanyaru River, F4
Biruruma River, D2
Bugarama, F1
Butare (Astrida), E3
Byumba, C4
Cyangugu, E1
Cyesha, E1
Dendezi, E3
Gabiro (Nyarugumba), B5
Gahini, C6
Gako, D4

Gatsibo, C5
Gatumba, D3
Gikongoro, E3
Gisenyi, C2
Gishyita, D2
Gitarama, D3
Kabaya, C3
Kabgayi, D3
Kagera National Park, C6
Kagera River, B5
Kagitumba River, B5
Kamababa River, D6

Kamembe, E1
Kazenze, D4
Kayonza, D5
Kibeho, F3
Kibungo (Birenga), D6
Kibuye, D2
Kigali, D4
Kiziguro, C5
Lake Burera, B3
Lake Cohoha-Sud, E4
Lake Hago, C6
Lake Ihema, D6
Lake Kivu, D1

Lake Mugesera, D5
Lake Muhazi, C5
Lake Ruhondo, C3
Lake Rwanye, B5
Lake Rwehikama, D6
Lake Rweru, E5
Luhwa River, E1
Mont Nemba, E4
Mount Karisimbi, B2
Mugambazi, C4
Mukungwa River, C3
Muramba, D2

Mwogo River, E3
Nguzi, D6
Ntendezi, E1
Nyabarongo River, D4
Nyakarambi, D6
Nyakatale, B5
Nyanza, E3
Ruhengeri, B3
Rusumo Falls, E6
Ruzizi River, E1
Sabinyo Volcano, B3
Taruka, C3
Virunga Range, C2

UGANDA
ZAÏRE
REPUBLIC
TANZANIA
Kagitumba
Sabinyo Volcano
Lake Burera
Nyakatale
Kagitumba River
Kagera River
Kagera River
Mount Karisimbi
Ruhengeri
Lake Ruhondo
Byumba
Gabiro (Nyarugumba)
Lake Rwanye
VIRUNGA RANGE
Taruka (Hydro Plant)
Gatsibo
KAGERA NATIONAL PARK
Gisenyi
Mukungwa River
Lake Hago
Kabaya
Mugambazi
Kiziguro
Lake Muhazi
Lake Ihema
Gatumba
Nyabarongo River
Gahini
Kamababa River
Lake Kivu
KIGALI
Kayonza
Kibuye
Gitarama
Nyabarongo River
Gishyita
Kabgayi
Kanzenze
Lake Rwehikama
Muramba
Biruruma River
Lake Mugesera
Nguzi
Gako
Kibungo (Birenga)
Cyesha
Mwogo River
Nyanza
Nyakarambi
Kamembe
Ntendezi
Dendezi
Mont Nemba
Lake Rweru
Cyangugu
Possible source of the Nile River
Gikongoro
Kagera River
Rusumo Falls
Kirehe
Lake Cohoha Sud
Ruzizi River
Luhwa River
Butare (Astrida)
Akanyaru River
Kibeho
Bugarama
ZAÏRE REPUBLIC
BURUNDI
N
RWANDA
TANZANIA
D
E
F
G
1 2 3 4 5 6

Mist gathers in the mountains near the Ruzizi valley.

region, and the altitude of the land ranges from twenty-six hundred feet to six thousand feet above sea level.

THE CENTRAL PLATEAUS

East of the mountains making up the Congo-Nile dividing crest is the area called the central plateaus. The plateaus are actually a region of rolling hills that become gradually lower as they near the eastern border.

In ancient times these hills were covered with forests. Man has long since destroyed the trees, and the land has been heavily farmed and grazed. In times of heavy rains, many mountain streams rush down these hills. Unfortunately, these streams carry away much soil, because the natural protectors of the soil—trees and grass—have been destroyed.

The climate of the hilly plateaus is very pleasant. The average temperature is about sixty-five degrees Fahrenheit, and

14

Cattle and herders at a river in the hills of Rwanda.

there are approximately fifty inches of rain each year. Such an agreeable climate is quite remarkable for a country situated deep in the tropics, not far from the equator.

THE SAVANNAS

The central plateau area slopes off into the savannas and swamps of the eastern part of Rwanda. A *savanna* is a grassy plain with bushes and a few trees; it is green when there is rain, but is a parched, wheat color during the dry season.

The east is drier and hotter than the central plateaus. Altitude averages about forty-two hundred feet above sea level. In some places, there may be no rain for up to six months of the year; these areas become semideserts. When the rains finally come, they may dump as much as thirty inches of water on the land. These "gifts" of water are so irregular that they do not change

15

the semidesert character that the land has most of the year. These rains, however, create many lakes and marshes among the semiarid areas of the southeast.

NATIONAL BOUNDARIES

The borders of Rwanda are still almost identical to the ones drawn in colonial times. In the late nineteenth century, Rwanda became part of German East Africa. The Germans arranged some of the borders in agreements with European countries that had neighboring colonies. Other parts of the borders were drawn by the Germans alone to mark separate areas within their own colonies.

The northern border with Uganda starts in the volcanic Virunga Range of northwestern Rwanda and goes eastward. It is often marked by small rivers, and it ends at the junction of the Kagitumba and Kagera rivers. Several roads cross the Rwanda-Uganda border, and people frequently move across the border in both directions.

The eastern border with Tanzania follows the Kagera River valley. The midpoint of the river is frequently the borderline. Where the border does not follow the river, it is clearly marked with stone pillars. Much of this border area is swampy and sparsely populated. No really important roads cross this boundary.

The southern border with Burundi dates from colonial times. Germany, which never had more than loose control over the area, viewed Rwanda and Burundi as more or less a unit. Even during the period of German control, however, the people knew where Rwanda stopped and Burundi began. After World War II, the United Nations formally recognized a border between Rwanda and Burundi. When the two countries became independent in 1962, they accepted that same border.

The border follows the Kagera, Akanyaru, and Luhwa rivers, which flow east to west; it crosses lakes Rugwero and Cohoha-Sud. Spaces between bodies of water are divided by artificial lines. The border ends where the Luhwa and Ruzizi rivers meet. An important road crosses the central part of the southern border, connecting Kigali, capital of Rwanda, with Bujumbura, capital of Burundi.

Along Rwanda and Burundi's short, western border is another road. This road connects the people who live around each country's great lake, Lake Kivu in Rwanda and Lake Tanganyika, which touches a small strip of Burundi. In addition to the roads, many trails cross the Rwanda-Burundi borders. The populations of the two countries are made up of the same peoples. To a great extent they share a common history, and in language and custom they are much alike.

Fishermen at night on one of Rwanda's many lakes.

Three Children of Rwanda

ROBERT AT KAGERA NATIONAL PARK

Robert (pronounced *roh BAIR*) had seen it first. He had scrambled up to the top of the hill ahead of the others. As the three men reached the top, Robert was pointing off into the distance.

There it was, just where he was pointing: smoke!

One of the men had binoculars slung around his neck. He raised them to his eyes for a closer look at the fire. Each of the men took a turn with the glasses. They were trying to decide exactly where the fire was. In a few minutes, they had agreed on its location. Then they hurried back to their truck.

From the top of the hill, Robert could see a giraffe in the forest below.

Robert ran all the way back to the truck. He did not want to keep anyone waiting, since he was a guest with the park rangers and anxious not to be any trouble.

Most of the year Robert goes to school near the town of Kigali. He thinks books are much less interesting than animals. Robert finds it hard to sit in school; he would rather be out in the country where the animals are. He knows, though, that to be a park ranger he will have to finish school.

Not too long ago he learned about the college of African Wildlife Management, where people learn how to protect animals. The school is in a Tanzanian town called Mossi, near the border. Since the day his teacher mentioned the school, Robert has wanted to go there. He has already made up his mind that, if necessary, he will walk to the school.

Robert's brother Alphonse is a park ranger at Kagera National Park. Because he knew that Robert was so interested in becoming a park ranger, he gave Robert permission to spend his vacation in the park, working with the rangers. Robert was having a great time in the park. He was trying very hard to be useful to the rangers so they would let him return during his next vacation.

At their camp, Robert was caring for two baby antelopes that the rangers had found alone and afraid in the woods. Their mother had probably been killed and eaten by a lion. At first, Robert fed them canned milk mixed with water. They did not know how to drink; so he started by dipping his thumb in the milk and letting them suck the milk off the thumb. Since that was a very slow process, he rolled a rag, soaked it in the milk, and let them suck it. Soon

the young antelope were drinking milk from a can and eating leaves. Robert had decided that he would turn them loose near a herd of antelope when they were a little bigger.

The three men were on patrol this morning, just as they were almost every day, when they spotted the smoke. Smoke was one of the signs they had been looking for, since smoke meant that there were poachers (illegal hunters) in the park. Sometimes poachers worked in groups. Then the smoke might come from a ring of fire that the poachers set to drive the animals past their guns or spears. The smoke might also come from the cooking fire of some lone hunter. Whatever its cause, the fire might spread and destroy the forest; so it had to be put out.

The three men jumped into the cabin of their little truck. Robert was already in the back. Leaving behind a trail of red dust, they sped along the dirt road in the direction of the smoke. In the back of the truck, Robert bounced all the way there. He didn't care, though, because he was happy that he had been allowed to come along.

After about ten minutes the truck stopped. Everybody got out and started to walk across the country. Each time they reached the top of a hill, they could see that they were nearer to the smoke. Luckily, there was not much of it.

Finally, they approached the grove of trees from which the smoke was coming. They spread out and quietly slipped closer. What they found was a single fire;

*Robert knew that when his young antelope were bigger,
he would turn them loose near a herd of antelope like these.*

beside it, an old man and woman were eating a small animal they had cooked. The old people were frightened to see the rangers.

Alphonse told them sternly that hunting was forbidden in the park, but they did not seem to understand. Their family had roamed and hunted there long before it was a park. Neither the man nor the woman had ever been to school; naturally, they were puzzled by this talk of laws that forbade them to catch their food as they always had.

Alphonse explained, more gently now, why the fire was dangerous. Quickly, the old man and woman put it out. The rangers let them go. Alphonse gave them the cooked meat that was left. "There is no sense in wasting it," he said, "but you must go out of the park to hunt."

"They will never really understand why we chase them from the park," said Alphonse. "That's sad, but what is more important is that people your age, Robert, are learning to protect our animals."

JEAN AT THE NYABARONGO RIVER

Jean (pronounced *ZHAHN*) thought this must be the happiest day of his life.

He and his brother were walking through weeds in water above their knees, pushing a new canoe.

The canoe was Jean's. He and his father had carved it from a tree trunk. Because of Jean's school and his father's work, they had not had much time to work on it; so it had taken a long time to finish. Jean was happy that at last it was ready and he and his brother could go fishing in it.

Jean's family lives near the Nyabarongo River and several lakes. Fishing is what Jean enjoys most. He knows how to fish with a spear, a line, or a net. Until he had a canoe of his own, though, he had to fish from his uncle's canoe or from the shore.

When the water was getting close to the boy's waists, they climbed into the canoe. They were almost through the reeds now, near open water. In a few minutes, they would arrive at the spot where they wanted to fish.

Today Jean was going to use his net. He, his father, and his brother had made that, too. First they had twisted fibers from plants into string. Then they plaited the string into a net. At some places, they carefully fastened stones right into the net. The weight of the stones would make the net sink.

When they came to the place they had chosen to fish, Jean's brother took over the

Before Jean had a canoe of his own, he often fished from the shore or a bridge.

paddling. Skillfully, he kept the canoe almost motionless in the water while Jean stood up, holding the carefully folded net. With one motion, he flung the net away from the boat and over the water. Keeping hold of the drawstrings at one end of the net, he let the weights carry the net down. He waited a little while, then slowly began to pull on the drawstrings. This motion closed the net; when it was completely closed, he pulled it up to the boat. There was nothing in it.

Jean pulled the net out of the water and started again. Time after time, as the canoe moved very slowly along, he cast his net. Usually the net was empty when he pulled it in, but occasionally it held a fish, and sometimes even two. In about two hours, there were a dozen small fish in the bottom of the boat. This would be plenty for dinner for the whole family.

Pleased with their work, they started home. They knew their mother would meet them with a big smile.

Jean let his canoe and the fish dry in the sun before returning home.

Jean had learned at school that fish was an excellent food. The teacher had told her class that the government wanted people to eat fish for better nourishment. Jean and his family loved to eat fish, but he knew that many Rwandans had never eaten fish and did not even care to try it. He wondered how the government could persuade these people to eat fish. Perhaps, when he was older he would help. He pictured himself an adult with a family of his own living near Lake Mugasera. He liked to imagine himself and his children in many canoes—just like his new one—with nets full of fish.

In the meantime, Jean planned to fertilize his family's corn crops. He had read a book about the United States of America which described how the Indians had taught the colonists to fertilize corn crops by planting fish with the seeds. Jean knew his family wouldn't have any extra whole fish that he could use, so he was going to put the leftovers—tails, fins, and bones—into their family corn plot at seed time. If it worked, he would have something really interesting to tell his teacher.

GHISELE RETURNS TO KIGALI

Ghisele watched the hills of Rwanda tilt as her Air Zaïre plane banked over the airport at Kigali. As the plane began its approach to the airstrip, the hills seemed to slip back into place.

Looking out the airplane window, Ghisele realized that she was happy to be home. Rwanda was very beautiful. Even though she knew Rwanda was really a crowded country, it looked quite empty to her now. That was partly because she was coming from New York, along with her mother and her brother.

Ghisele's father works for the Mission of Rwanda at the United Nations (UN). She and her family live in Manhattan, right in the middle of New York City. Ghisele goes to a special school for United Nations children. No wonder that, coming back to Rwanda for the first time in a year, the country looked empty!

Below, she could see a number of cars parked at the airport. She tried to pick out the one that belonged to her uncle, who would meet Ghisele and her family at the airport.

Ghisele giggled a little when she thought of trying to pick out a car from all the cars at Kennedy International Airport in New York. There had seemed to be millions of people and cars there when they left New York two days before.

Though Kennedy International Airport was exciting, Ghisele thought that small airports were nicer in some ways. At Kennedy Ghisele's dog was put into a special traveling box; he had to ride in the baggage compartment of the big jet. This morning at the airport in Bujumbura, Burundi, the Air Zaïre hostess had let her take their dog into the plane with them. She just had to promise to keep him at her seat.

The plane was on the runway now. Since it was the only plane arriving that day, there were not very many people at the airport. Ghisele's uncle was waiting at the foot of the stairs when the family came out of the airplane. A few minutes later, they were all in his car on the way to their grandmother's house at Gitarama.

During the ride Ghisele planned her summer. First of all, she would do her school homework. Her teacher had given the students two assignments; the first assignment was to bring back two objects made by people in their native countries.

Ghisele knew what she would bring. She was going to ask one of her other uncles to make her a *lulunga,* a musical instrument with eight strings. In Rwanda someone in almost every family can play one. In New York a woman once came to their school and played a harp for the pupils. Ghisele thought it sounded much like a lulunga.

She planned to go over to her uncle's house and watch him work on the lulunga. She hoped he would teach her to play at least one easy piece, so she could demonstrate it for her class.

She also planned to take several woven baskets and bowls to school. At home Ghisele's family used many utensils made of black-and-white raffia and millet straw.

The second homework assignment would be a little harder, but it would be fun, too. Each student in her class had made a list of some of the sayings or proverbs of his country. All the students then exchanged lists.

During the summer, each child was to match each saying on his list with one from his own country. The sayings could have the same meanings or opposite ones.

Ghisele had received the list of an American boy. She laughed when she read it. She had never heard many of the sayings before, at least not in the United States, but she had heard sayings much like some of these in Rwanda.

Almost as soon as she saw her grandmother, Ghisele told her about the assignment. Her grandmother wanted to know about the proverbs from the faraway land.

" 'One bad apple can spoil the barrel,' " she said.

Her grandmother smiled and said, "When we mean that, we say, 'You do not tie a bad goat near yours.' "

Ghisele said, "What about, 'Two heads are better than one?' "

"Almost exactly the same," said her grandmother, "as the Rwandan expression, 'One head cannot give advice.' "

"Try this one," said Ghisele. " 'Too many cooks spoil the broth.' "

"That's easy. In Rwanda you would say, 'Many hunters miss the dogs' tracks.' Now let's try it the other way around. What would Americans say for 'A small pot is good when there is no other?' "

Ghisele tried hard to think of something. Her mother answered quickly, " 'Half a loaf is better than none.' "

Now everybody joined in. When Ghisele suggested "A new broom sweeps clean," her uncle immediately came up with "New handles cause callouses." They

On the way to Gitarama Ghisele saw many peasants at work in their fields.

all began to argue about that answer, since Ghisele's proverb seemed to mean that it is good to change, while her uncle's meant that change was difficult.

Ghisele then thought of another. " 'However you make your bed, you must lie in it,' " she suggested.

Several people answered in unison: " 'He who makes the beer has to drink it.' "

"You know," said her grandmother, laughing, "these Americans sound very sensible. There must be a Rwandan in their family somewhere."

27

A group of royal dancers.

Rwanda Yesterday

EARLY RESIDENTS

The first people known to have lived in Rwanda were the Twa. They are related to the pygmies, the earliest inhabitants of east-central Africa. The early Twa lived in the forests. They did not farm, but lived by hunting and gathering food such as nuts and roots. They were good warriors and excellent musicians and dancers. Eventually, many of the Twa retreated deeper into the forests to get away from the Hutu, the next people to come to Rwanda.

The Hutu are a Bantu people. The word Bantu describes a black-skinned people who live in equatorial and southern Africa and speak one of a group of related tongues called Bantu. Very little is known about the origins of the Hutu except that they probably came from the north. The Hutu were farmers. To make room for farming, they began to clear away the forests that covered much of Rwanda.

The Hutu established small kingdoms. Their kings were called *bahinza,* which means "those who can make things grow." The people believed that the bahinza had magic powers to make rain and to protect crops.

No one knows exactly when the Hutu came to the area, but their many, tiny kingdoms were already well established five or six hundred years ago. It was about that time that the Tutsi, the most recent arrivals, began moving into Rwanda. The Tutsi came from somewhere to the northeast of Rwanda. The Tutsi are Nilotic: they are one of the groups of people who originated near the Nile River.

The Tutsi were wandering herdsmen and warriors. They did not all come to Rwanda at once; they came in groups, wandering south into the country over a period of years. Some of them went beyond Rwanda into Burundi. Though there were far fewer Tutsi than Hutu in the area, in time both Rwanda and Burundi became Tutsi kingdoms.

THE RULERS

The Tutsi believed that they were born to be rulers. Legend, carefully preserved by the Tutsi kings' chroniclers (record keepers), describes the beginning of Tutsi rule.

The legend tells of three children born in "the north" (what Westerners think of as heaven): two brothers, Kigwa and Mututsi, and a girl, Nyampundu. By accident, the three children fell to earth. They brought with them fire, iron, the forge, and cattle. Kigwa married Nyampundu and founded the first Tutsi family. One of the descendants was Gihanga, whose name means "founder." The legend says that it was Gihanga who led the Tutsi into Rwanda. According to this tradition, Gihanga's son, Kanyarwanda, was the first *mwami,* or king, of Rwanda.

Though this legend gives an explanation for the Tutsi control of Rwanda, it was really through the use of weapons and the control of cattle that the Tutsi were able to conquer the country. Professional warriors, the Tutsi were much more interested in fighting and had better weapons than the Hutu. The local bahinza and his men were amateurs compared to a Tutsi warrior band. Even so, the Tutsi conquest was neither easy nor quick. There were frequent wars for several centuries. Some of the fighting was among rival Tutsi groups, but most of it was Tutsi versus Hutu.

The Twa earned a privileged position in the eyes of the Tutsi. Because of their prowess in warfare, their excellent musical and dancing abilities, and their talent as court jesters, they were respected far more than the Hutu farmers. Occasionally brave Twa warriors were raised to the rank of Tutsi and given Tutsi wives.

Eventually the Tutsi mwami controlled most of the country, but no mwami ever completely controlled it. There always remained some Hutu-controlled areas in northwest Rwanda.

There were also frequent fights with Burundi. Even though their populations were of the same peoples—Hutu, Tutsi, and Twa—the two countries became traditional enemies.

UBUHAKE

The Tutsi used weapons to enlarge their kingdom, but they used cattle to gain the upper hand in daily life with the Hutu. The Tutsi had brought herds of cattle with them to Rwanda. Since most Hutu did not own cattle but very much wanted to do so, bargains were made. The Tutsi loaned some of their cattle to Hutu people, who cared for the cattle and kept the milk and some of the calves. In return, the Hutu gave the Tutsi produce from their farms and whatever labor they needed.

Each side got something it wanted from the bargain. If a Hutu took good care of the cattle entrusted to him, he could one day have a herd of his own. Unlike the Hutu, the Tutsi despised farming. By lending their cattle, they freed themselves from the need to do any manual labor.

What started as a simple exchange—a cow for vegetables and work—became the way of life in the entire country. The Tutsi became powerful local lords, and the Hutu became peasants bound to these lords. A Hutu man worked his lord's fields, repaired his houses, and carried him in a kind of hammock when he traveled. The agreement between the owner and the user of cattle was called *ubuhake;* it was similar to the feudal system of Europe in the Dark Ages. Each particular agreement did not end with the deaths of the men who made it. Instead, the obligations of ubuhake were inherited by their sons.

Ubuhake agreements were made not only between Hutu and Tutsi. Tutsi who had fewer cattle or less power sometimes entered into such agreements with other richer and stronger Tutsi. For them,

A Tutsi warrior.

The whole kingdom was organized on the system of ubuhake, where the Hutu cared for the Tutsi cattle. Today many Hutu have their own cattle, generally cared for by young boys.

ubuhake was more of an alliance between weaker and stronger; between Hutu and Tutsi it was closer to the relationship of master and servant. When the agreement was between two Tutsi men, the weaker of the two did not give physical labor in return for the cattle and protection. Instead, he fought for his lord when there was a war, accompanied him when he traveled, and gave advice and support in Tutsi quarrels and rivalries.

The whole kingdom came to be organized on the basis of ubuhake. Just as in the feudal society of Europe during the Middle Ages, the weaker attached themselves to the stronger. At the head of the society was the most powerful lord, the mwami. All of the other lords owed him their allegiance.

The mwami's ancestors were believed to have come from "the north" (from what Westerners think of as heaven). The mwami was described as "the eye through which God looks on Rwanda." The symbol of the mwami's power was not a throne or a crown, but a sacred drum, the *kalinga*.

The mwami had a council of "great chiefs" who were his advisers. Each great chief was also in charge of one section of the kingdom. Under every great chief was a cattle chief (Tutsi) and a land chief (Hutu). These two chiefs collected the tribute—cattle and farm produce—that was owed to the mwami by their district. In theory, the mwami was the true owner of all land and all cattle. There were also military chiefs who were in charge of the kingdom's frontier areas. The military chiefs had two jobs: to conduct cattle raids across the borders and to guard the borders from invaders.

THE COLONIZERS

The kingdom of Rwanda remained isolated from most of the rest of the world until less than one hundred years ago. The ancient Romans and Egyptians, and the Arab traders, however, had known about Rwanda and might have drawn upon its wealth to a small extent. Rwanda was isolated partly because the country was remote and difficult to reach across its mountains and swamps. Rwandans took advantage of their remoteness to live by themselves, and rumors from the people who lived near their borders gave the Rwandans a reputation as fierce fighters who did not welcome uninvited guests.

Their carefully guarded isolation was of great benefit to the Rwandans. They were not carried off into slavery, since the Arab slave traders could not enter Rwanda. Arab slave traders did make many attempts to penetrate Rwanda, but they were driven off by the powerful bow-and-arrow warfare of the Tutsi, who had the advantage of being able to shoot downhill.

No European had yet seen Rwanda in 1884 when the governments of Europe held the Berlin Conference. This conference was called so the European countries could divide Africa among themselves. At the meeting, it was decided that

Burundi and Rwanda would be a German "sphere of interest." This meant that the Germans had first choice on colonizing and developing the area. It was not until nine years later, however, that a German explorer, Count von Goetzen, became the first European to visit Rwanda.

Some European explorers had come to the edges of Rwanda before this time. In 1855 John Speke and Sir Richard Burton, two British explorers, came near Rwanda while searching for the sources of the Nile River. Speke was also at the edge of the country in 1861, and Henry Stanley was there in 1876.

Toward the end of the 1890s, officials in German East Africa managed to extend their control loosely into Rwanda. In 1899 Germany made Rwanda and Burundi part of German East Africa (which already included the large territory of Tanganyika). A German military post was established at Kigali in 1907 and a prominent German explorer and scientist, Richard Kandt, was named resident (governor) of Rwanda.

The Germans, who sent very few people to Africa, tried to rule Rwanda indirectly. Their plan was to control the mwami and the queen mother, who ruled jointly with the mwami until independence. The mwami and queen mother would control the people. The system of cattle chief and land chief for each district was abandoned. The mwami in power at that time, Yuhi Musinga, was eager to use the German troops to strengthen his power. German expeditions attacked the groups on Rwanda's borders that had been resisting the mwami's control. During the time of German colonization, Musinga came closer than had any other mwami to having complete control of his country.

While Rwanda was under their control, the Germans attempted three major projects: to introduce coffee as a cash crop, to take a census of the African population, and to educate some of the people.

Until about 1913 people had traded goods they had for goods they wanted, in what was called the *barter system*. The Germans introduced coffee growing in 1913, and a money economy came into existence as the coffee crop began to be sold outside the country.

The census was difficult to take accurately. The Germans had each chief report on how many huts were in his area, and in 1911 the African population of Rwanda was estimated at about two million.

Education was handled by Christian missionaries, who were supposed to train some of the Tutsi so they could work for the Germans in the government. The missionaries also educated some Hutu, which gave these individuals the potential for a higher status—sometimes an educated or wealthy Hutu could persuade a poor Tutsi to give a daughter in marriage.

BELGIAN ADMINISTRATION

German plans for Rwanda were barely under way when World War I began in

Three Tutsi chiefs.

PHOTOS ON THESE PAGES COURTESY OF INFOR-CONGO

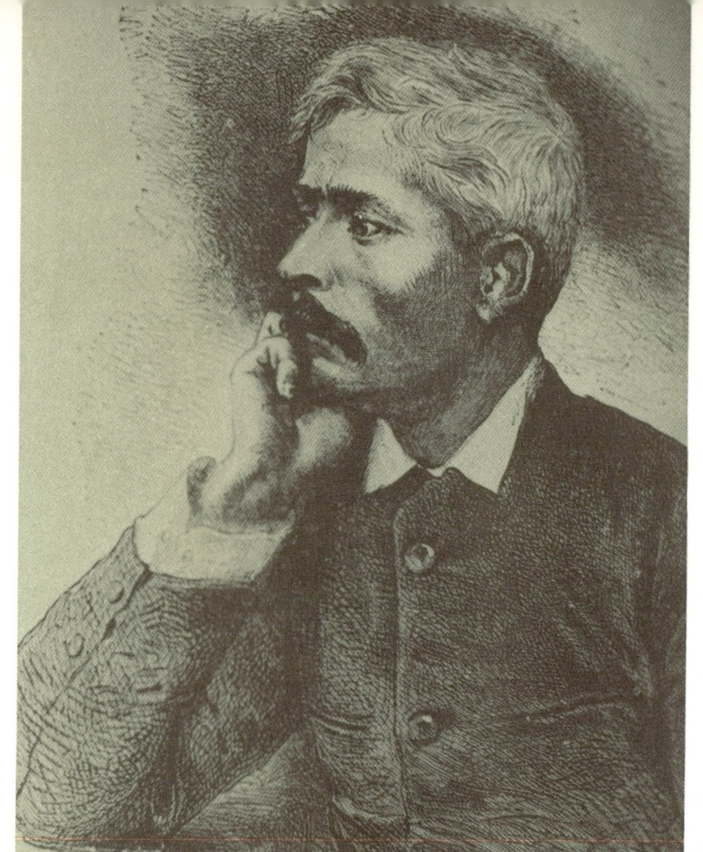

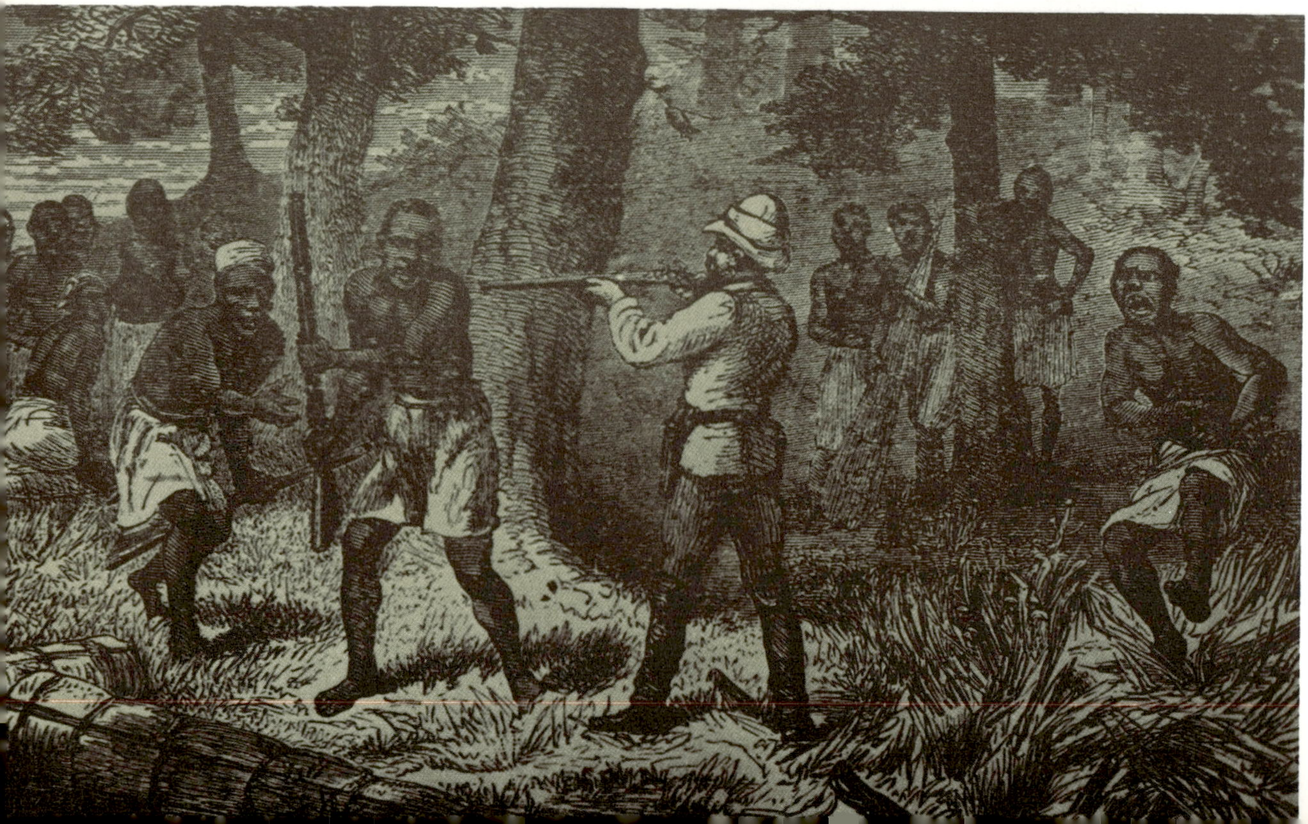

Henry Stanley (above left) came near Rwanda in the mid-1800s while searching for the source of the Nile River. Below left: Stanley stops a mutiny. Above: Stanley cuts his way through the dangerous forest.

The Belgians planted many crops in the valleys of Rwanda. Left: A banana plantation. Right: On each banana plant grow flower buds. A bract (like a heavy petal) rolls back from the bud, exposing small flowers, some of which become tiny, green bananas.

Europe. Germany was at war with England, France, Portugal, and Belgium. The few German troops in Rwanda and Burundi were far outnumbered by Belgian forces just across the border in the Belgian Congo (now called Zaïre). In May of 1916 the Germans were defeated in the battle against the Belgians; the Belgians then took over the territories of Rwanda and Burundi.

The Belgian government did not intend to keep these territories. It hoped that when the war was over the European countries would trade some of their colonies in Africa. Belgium would have been pleased to give up Rwanda and Burundi; in exchange, it wanted a piece of land on the southern bank of the lower Congo River.

Belgium was disappointed in its hope for a swap; instead, in 1923 Rwanda and Burundi together became a mandated territory of the League of Nations. The league had been set up shortly after World War I in hopes of avoiding any future world conflicts. Much like the United Nations did after World War II, the League of Nations supervised many territories around the world whose ownership was in dispute due to the results of World War I. The idea was to protect people who were not able to protect themselves.

Belgium was given direct control of Rwanda and Burundi. The Belgians were obliged, according to their agreement with the League of Nations, to maintain peace, order, and good administration in the territory. It was their duty to provide modern education and health care, as well as to promote the progress and well-being of the African population. To make the Belgians' task easier, the League of

Nations allowed them to run the territory as part of the Belgian Congo (now Zaïre). Many foreigners came to think of both Rwanda and Burundi merely as two provinces of the Congo.

In Rwanda the Belgians concentrated most of all on food production. The high population density (an average of 373 people per square mile) and the large amount of land not suitable for cultivation had contributed to the food supply problem. Because not enough food was raised to last from one season to the next, there were famines in Rwanda each year. The Belgians worked to help the Rwandans plant crops in the relatively wet valleys during the dry season; these crops provided extra food. Also, the Belgians helped the people raise crops that could be exported to other countries; these crops helped the economy.

After World War II, The League of Nations was replaced by a new, international organization, the United

The Belgians introduced medical facilities and education in Rwanda. Below: An African is treated by a doctor. Right: Children are taught how to brush their teeth.

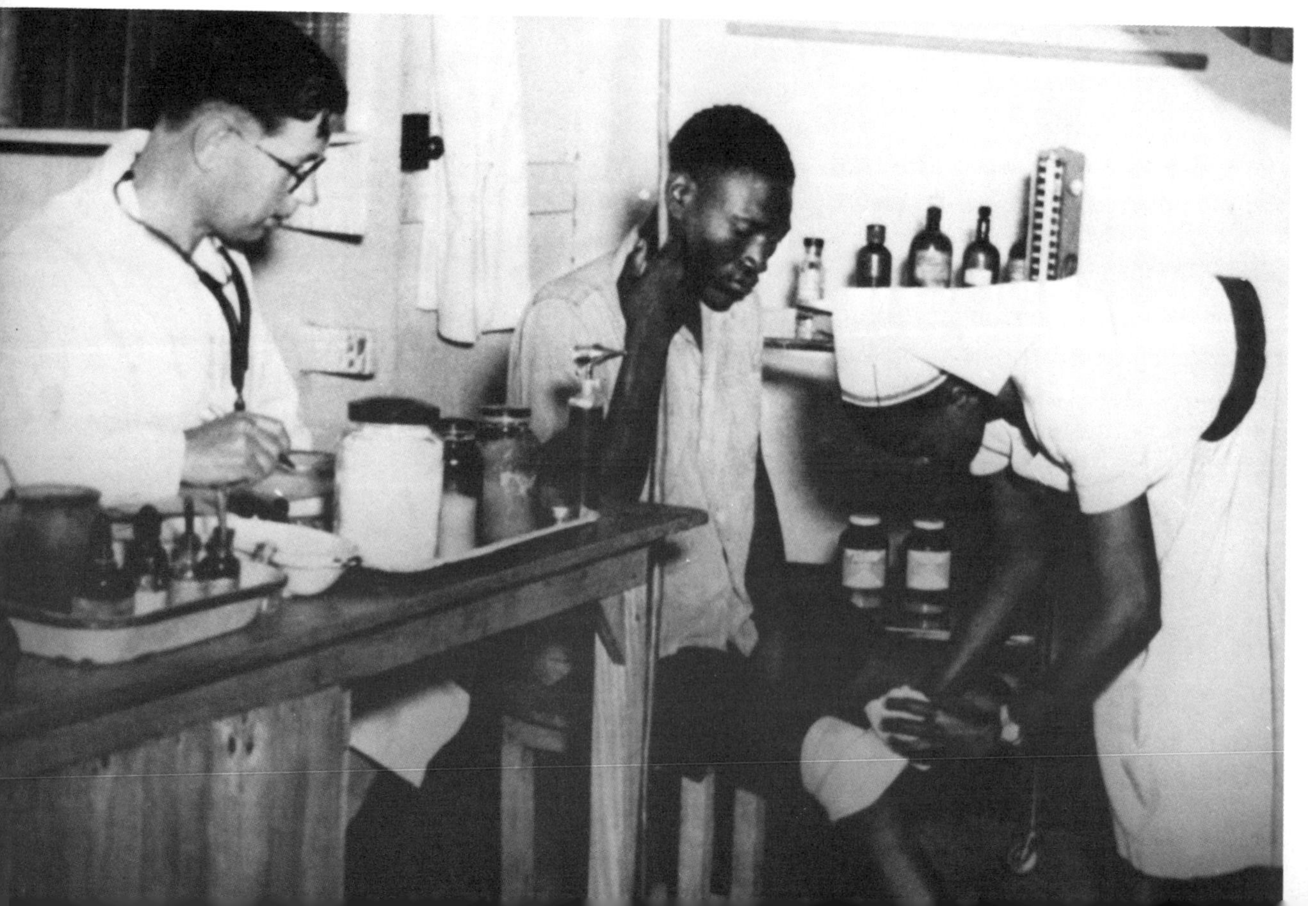

Nations (UN). Rwanda and Burundi had been a mandated territory under the League of Nations; now they were made a UN Trust Territory, under the name Ruanda-Urundi, with Belgium still continuing to administer the territory.

The United Nations gave Belgium a new task in addition to the ones it had under the league. The Belgian government was still obliged to maintain peace and promote the well-being of the people. Now it was also required to work for the political development of the people by ridding the country of its old, feudal ways. Belgium was asked to prepare both Ruanda and Urundi for self-government.

Belgium would be training the people to run a country that was no longer an isolated little kingdom, but part of the large and modern world. The Belgian government accepted the United Nations trusteeship agreement in 1946, and Ruanda started the last stage of its journey back to independence.

UNITED NATIONS

Rwanda Today

PREPARING FOR INDEPENDENCE

During the thirteen years that Ruanda-Urundi was a UN Trust Territory, there was constant disagreement between Belgium and the UN Trusteeship Council.

The Belgians felt that worthwhile political development could come only after economic and social progress. They said: "First more food, medicine, and schools; then we'll worry about giving the people the opportunity to govern themselves." The UN Trusteeship Council wanted immediate political development. It said: "Work toward government by the people themselves at the same time you work for more schools, food, and medicine."

The Trusteeship Council several times sent inspectors to Ruanda-Urundi. Urged on by their reports, Belgium speeded up efforts at political development. In 1952 members of the advisory councils at various levels of government began to be elected rather than appointed. Elections first held in 1953 gave the minority Tutsi control over the councils. At the same time the Belgian government put into effect a Ten-Year Plan for Ruanda-Urundi. This plan would improve the schools and the living conditions and bring the people closer to self-government. The councils at different levels of government that had been set up in 1943 to advise the mwami were expanded. Though the represen-

People walk into a village for the celebration of Rwanda's independence.

tatives to these councils had always been chosen by the mwami, some could now be elected.

In 1954 the High Council decided to end the practice of ubuhake. In the next four years, two hundred thousand head of cattle were divided among people who became their owners, not just their guardians. Since the Hutu were the majority and since they had owned the fewest cattle, they gained most. They did not gain equality with the Tutsi, however, for the pasturelands were still primarily controlled by the Tutsi. Still, the end of ubuhake changed the mood of the country. The Hutu now realized that if they could get a share of the cattle, they could also get a share of the land.

In 1956 all adult males were given the right to choose the people who would elect the various advisory councils. The following year, the High Council, whose members were all Tutsi, called for immediate training in modern government for people who had already been to European-type schools. Most of the graduates of foreign schools were Tutsi. The Hutu feared that if the High Council's desire for independence was met quickly, the Tutsi would again control the country.

United Nations representatives who visited Ruanda at this time may have been slightly confused by the mixture of political banners and slogans that greeted them. Some read, "Immediate Independence! Get Rid Of The Belgians For Us!" Others said, "Down with Tutsi Feudalism! Long Live Belgian Trusteeship!"

Political organizations began to be formed. Among these were the Hutu Social Movement and the Association for the Social Betterment of the Masses (APROSOMA). Both were Hutu organizations that began in 1957. In January of 1959 APROSOMA became a political party; in September of that year, the Rwanda National Union Party (UAR) was formed by Tutsi whose goal was independence in 1962 under a constitutional monarchy. In October the Hutu Social Movement was transformed into the Party of the Hutu Emancipation Movement (PARMEHUTU).

Differences became bitter, and late in 1959 fighting broke out between Hutu and Tutsi. Thousands of people were killed, most of them Tutsi. Many Tutsi went into exile in neighboring countries.

After much further dispute, elections for the Legislative Assembly, which would be the national congress, were held in October, 1961. Originally, these elections had been scheduled for January of 1961, but they were postponed because of the fighting. The United Nations supervised the elections. The Hutu parties received 80 percent of the vote, and the same overwhelming majority voted to end the monarchy. The new Legislative Assembly quickly declared a republic. All the mwami's authority was removed. Gregoire Kayibanda was elected president by the Assembly.

On July 1, 1962, Ruanda's independence became official. The country's name was then changed to Rwanda.

*Independence Day. School children hold flags
of the newly proclaimed Republic of Rwanda.*

Independence Day. Right: The arch built to welcome visitors. Children parade (below) and the National Guard stand at attention (far right), while the flag is raised at a ceremony in Kigali.

A TRUE FATHER OF HIS COUNTRY

Grégoire Kayibanda was thirty-nine years old when he became president of Rwanda. That is not a remarkably young age for a national leader in Africa, since many younger men hold high office in newly independent countries.

As were most Hutu leaders, Kayibanda was educated in a Roman Catholic seminary. At that time, the seminary offered the best chance for a good education, since subjects such as French, typing, filing, and teaching were offered. Many seminary graduates worked as clerks for government officials, while others went on to become politically active.

The young Kayibanda worked for a few years as a primary school teacher; later he edited a newspaper. In 1957 he founded the Hutu Social Movement.

Kayibanda is a very popular president. He is revered by the Hutu as the leader in their struggle against the Tutsi. As president, Kayibanda has kept his simple way of life, refusing to own big cars and expensive houses. He is a quiet, deeply serious man. President Kayibanda hopes to lead his people not only to prosperity, but also to his own high ideal of life.

In 1965 and 1969, Kayibanda was the only candidate for president. He received over 90 percent of the votes each time.

THE GOVERNMENT

The constitution of Rwanda provides for a government with three branches. The president is the chief executive and head of the armed forces. He appoints a Council of Ministers and each minister runs one

department of the government; in 1969 there were twelve ministers. The president also appoints many government officials, including the members of the Supreme Court.

The National Assembly is the legislative branch of the government and is composed of forty-seven members. The members of the Assembly elect a president, vice-president, and secretary-general of the Assembly from among their own members. Both the Assembly and the executive branch of government can initiate bills.

The Supreme Court decides whether laws are constitutional before they are put into effect. When the Assembly passes a law, it goes to both the president and the Constitutional Court. The Constitutional Court determines whether the law fits the standards set down by the national constitution. This court is made up of the same judges who make up the Supreme Court.

There are lower courts throughout the land to hear ordinary cases, but few of these cases are appealed to higher courts. Most of Rwanda's civil and criminal laws are based on Belgian law.

All Rwandans are eligible to vote from the age of eighteen. Voting is not only a right but a duty as well. Only people who have been convicted of murder, assassination, treason, or desertion from the army are forbidden to vote. Members of the military and police may not vote either, but may resume voting when they leave these organizations. All elected offices have four-year terms.

The country is divided into ten provinces, called *prefectures*. Each prefecture is named for the town that serves as its administrative center: Butare, Byumba, Cyangugu, Gikongoro, Gisenyi, Gitarama, Kibungo, Kibuye, Kigali, and Ruhengeri. The prefectures are divided into 141

RWANDA
PREFECTURES

communes, or local administrative areas. The prefectures are not very important to the structure of Rwanda's government; most administration is handled in Kigali, the national capital.

EDUCATION

Until the coming of the Europeans, Rwandan children were educated by their families. Children of both sexes below age five were taught proper behavior by their mothers. Older girls were instructed mostly by their mothers, and older boys by their fathers. From their earliest years, children learned strict ideas of good and bad from the many Rwandan folktales, proverbs, and songs. All of these taught respect and unquestioning loyalty and obedience toward one's superiors. Those who would become leaders were taught generosity, self-control, and language.

By the age of ten, Hutu boys were learning to farm and Hutu girls to do household chores. At the age of puberty Tutsi boys often left home to stay at the court of a great chief or even that of the mwami. There they learned public speaking, storytelling, and dancing, and were taught to develop qualities such as loyalty and generosity.

Roman Catholic and Protestant missionaries became established in Rwanda around 1900. Teaching people to read and write was one of the missionaries' main jobs. There were many "bush schools" in remote areas and a primary school at every mission station.

During the Belgian administration, the emphasis was on primary education. Missionaries were still in charge of education, but were partly supported by the government. Most of the pupils were Tutsi.

While Rwanda was a UN Trust Territory, primary schools were divided into two levels. The lower primary schools were taught in the Kinyarwanda language. Children studied hygiene, physical education, gardening, and such essential subjects as reading, writing, and arithmetic. Upper primary schools taught the same subjects, but emphasized manual training and agricultural subjects. The boys' upper schools also taught French, as did some of the girls' schools.

In 1929 a secondary school was founded by a group of Roman Catholic missionaries in what is now the town of Butare. This school also trained teachers and offered technical and vocational courses. It remained the only secondary school in Rwanda until the mid-1950s. In the years just before independence, more secondary, vocational, and teachers' training schools were established.

A gigantic effort in education began with independence. Since that time, the government of Rwanda has been spending one quarter of its budget each year for education. Most of this money is spent on primary schools. Still more money has come from missionaries and foreign aid, and is used for secondary and higher education. Both primary and secondary schools have been greatly expanded.

Children gather in front of their school.

The National University of Rwanda was established in 1963 by the government and the Catholic Dominican Order of Canada. It is in the town of Butare in southern Rwanda. Several hundred students study at the National University of Rwanda; more than a hundred Rwandans study at foreign universities.

Not far from the university is the Institute for Agricultural Sciences, where research on cultivating high-altitude crops and raising farm animals is carried on. There is also a veterinary laboratory here.

PRESS

Rwanda has two regular newspapers, one published in French and the other in Kinyarwanda. The periodical *Imvaho* is published in Kigali every two weeks. It reports current events in other countries as well as local news.

*This newly-built educational center includes a primary school,
a high school, and various technical schools.*

Kinyamateka is published weekly, in the Kinyarwanda language. It contains mostly Roman Catholic church news. One of its past editors is Grégoire Kayibanda, president of the republic.

Once a month *Rwanda Carrefour d'Afrique* (Rwanda Crossroads of Africa) is put out by the government's Ministry of Information and Tourism. Published in Kigali, it reports news of government programs and activities.

Together these three papers probably have an audience of half a million people. More than half the population of Rwanda cannot yet read, and more schools are being built to solve that problem. Meanwhile, people who cannot read are read to by those who can. Newspapers are often read to groups of people. Nearly fifty thousand people subscribe to at least one of the three papers, but ten times as many people probably hear them read.

UGANDA TOURIST BOARD

Natural Treasures

THE DESTRUCTION OF WILDLIFE

The wildlife of Africa is one of the world's great treasures. Nowhere else on earth is there anything to equal the variety and beauty of Africa's wild creatures. Wildlife is a natural treasure that human beings often squander. In almost every place that many people live, the animals, reptiles, birds, and fish have been driven out and often destroyed.

In the past two thousand years, 107 species of mammals have been wiped out. Much of the destruction is recent. Sixty-seven of these species have vanished in the last hundred years.

The destruction still continues and many species are threatened. The greatest danger to the animals is lack of space. Africa's cheetah, gorilla, and white rhinoceros, all of whom are native to Rwanda, are in danger of dying out.

African governments are trying to save their wildlife. Rwanda, home to many famous species, has a large reserve where animals roam freely. This reserve, Kagera National Park, is located on the northeastern border of Rwanda. It covers about one thousand square miles. Though Rwanda is the most densely populated country in Africa, it has reserved one-tenth of all its land in this protected homeland for animals.

About half a million wild creatures live in Kagera National Park. The environment needed by these animals is preserved

A lioness sits in the grass at a national park.

in the park by law. There the animals are protected against hunters, too. Only limited numbers of certain animals may be hunted in a specific hunting area and only by people with a special license.

Poachers (illegal hunters) are the park's biggest problem. They often kill small game to sell or eat. Poachers sometimes kill small antelope and gazelles to use as bait in trapping leopards, since leopard skins bring high prices in illegal sales. The horns of the rhinoceros are also smuggled across African borders. Ground to powder, they are then sold as medicine.

Elephants require much forest land for their migrations.

At the Kagera National Park, game wardens guard against poachers. Protecting animals is a difficult and expensive job, but virtually everyone who has seen the animals agrees that the job is worthwhile.

Another problem is preserving the forests. Thousands of acres of forest land are needed as feeding ground for the huge, migratory animals such as elephants, who feed on leaves and twigs. When elephants have finished feeding in a forest, they leave it, often not returning for years. Their migrations tend to follow large, circular patterns. These great beasts often travel hundreds of miles in migratory wanderings.

RWANDA'S MOST HUNTED ANIMAL

Elephants are surprisingly gentle and loving to each other. When one of their number has been attacked, others try to help him. They press against the wounded animal to keep him upright, helping him to escape from his attacker. Young elephants stand guard around old ones that are grazing, warning their elders of the approach of any danger.

Elephants have been known to rescue one of their kind trapped in a hunter's pit. To do this a group of elephants tramps down the ground at the side of the pit forming a ramp into the pit. The imprisoned elephant then simply walks out.

The most hunted animal has been the elephant. Hundreds of thousands of these wonderful creatures have been killed for their ivory tusks. Africans probably first carved and sold the tusks of elephants that had died naturally. As more traders came to Africa in the eighteenth and nineteenth centuries, people found that they could sell all the elephant tusks they could get. The great elephant hunt that developed soon became a slaughter.

Elephant hunters dug pits and covered them with light branches and leaves. Any elephant that stepped onto the trap was lost, since an elephant weighs five or six tons and cannot jump from even a very shallow pit.

Sometimes the hunters set a fire in a big ring around one or more elephants. As the flames closed in on them, the terrified animals tried to escape and were killed. At first the hunters used their traditional spears, but later, guns supplied by traders made the killing easier.

ANOTHER NATIVE ANIMAL

Still another of Africa's most famous animals is at home in Rwanda—the wild mountain gorilla. Mountain gorillas are the largest of the great apes, often weighing more than four hundred pounds. Because of the many stories about gorillas attacking humans, gorillas have always been thought of as ferocious and very dangerous.

Today only a few thousand mountain gorillas live in a rather small region of rain forest in central Africa. This area includes the border where three countries meet—Zaïre, Uganda, and Rwanda. The three governments have set aside part of this area as parkland, where the gorillas are protected by law. The law, however, is sometimes far from these mountains; there are many intrusions from poachers and herders.

The big gorillas were still much feared when an American, Dianne Fossey, began to study them in 1967. She worked from a mountain camp in the part of Albert National Park located in Rwanda. It took only a short time to learn that these so-called ferocious animals were actually gentle and rather timid. They are vegetarians; they eat leaves, vines, wild celery, and fruit. Even the peaceful gorilla, however, will fight if he feels threatened.

If the gorillas are not to become extinct, they must be protected. To protect the gorillas, human beings must have more precise information about them. How many gorillas are there? Exactly where do they live? Why do they move about in their migrations? The work of Dianne Fossey and others will help to answer these and other questions. The answers will help Rwanda preserve one of its important natural treasures.

MINERALS AND PLANTS

Most of Rwanda's minerals are located in an area extending from the Congo-Nile dividing crest east to near Kigali, the capital city. None of Rwanda's minerals are found in very large quantities. Some of the most important minerals include lithium phosphate, tin ore, tungsten ore, and small amounts of uranium ore and gold. Large quantities of methane gas that can be used as a power source are found in Lake Kivu. Beds of lava in the western and northwestern parts of Rwanda hold potassium compounds that can serve as fertilizers.

Hundreds of years ago, much of Rwanda was covered with forests. Farmers, herders, and hunters cut down so many of the trees that today only about three percent of Rwanda's land area can be called true forest land. Most of this land is located in three separate areas: the top of the Congo-Nile dividing crest; the volcanic Virunga Range; and Wahu Island in Lake Kivu. There are also some savanna woodlands in the east. The government has set up special laws to preserve the forests; when the forests are used, they serve mostly as fuel and for building construction.

Even though only 3 percent of the land is actual forest, this does not mean that there are no trees elsewhere in Rwanda. On the contrary, many hillsides are lush with vegetation. In the last twenty years, many shrubs and trees, such as eucalyptus, have been planted in central highland farm areas to control land erosion.

The chatter of a chimpanzee can always be heard in the forest.

F

The People Live in Rwanda

There are approximately 3.8 million people in Rwanda—about 373 people per square mile. Because people tend to live in areas where the climate and soil are best, the population is not spread evenly throughout the country. In some regions there are nearly 700 people per square mile, while other areas have hardly any people. Rwanda is the most densely populated country in Africa.

THE PEOPLES

The population is made up primarily of three different peoples. Each people has a distinct place in Rwanda's society, though each is of a different ethnic origin. In many African countries each group has its own customs and social class system. When these countries achieved independence, the new leaders were faced with uniting the country's peoples into one nation.

Rwanda has long had one society in which each of the three ethnic groups had its own position. Over the centuries, the three groups have come together to share language, customs, and religion. Rwanda already had a well-developed feudal system when the Europeans came.

Twa The first of the groups to come to Rwanda, the Twa are now the least

While drinking a bottle of soda pop, a boy gazes at the lake.

numerous. They are related to the pygmies, the first people known to have lived in east-central Africa. At slightly over five feet tall, the average Twa is bigger than a typical pygmy. The Twa, like the pygmies, have always preferred to live in the forest. When they can, they live by hunting and gathering wild food.

Today the Twa make up only about 1 percent of the population of Rwanda. Some Twa, however, have intermarried with the Tutsi. The Twa were important as soldiers and court jesters in the preindependence Tutsi-controlled government. Representatives of the Twa lived at the royal court and were always part of any important ceremony.

Today some Twa eke out livings in the small area of surviving forest. Those who live near the Tutsi and Hutu often work as potters and artisans.

Tutsi The Tutsi are the descendants of the wandering herders and warriors who came to Rwanda five or six hundred years ago.

In comparison with the other peoples of Rwanda, the Tutsi are tall and slender. Their average height is five feet, eight inches and their average weight is about 126 pounds. Some, of course, are taller—particularly some of the dancers of the former royal court of Rwanda, who average well over six feet. The dancers, however, are all from an unusually tall clan, or family group, within the Tutsi. Because they have such splendid figures and are remarkable dancers, they have become famous far beyond Africa and have created an image of the Tutsi as giants. That image is not accurate. Though some Tutsi surpass the six-foot mark, most do not reach it.

When Rwanda was a kingdom, virtually all of its high positions were held by Tutsi. They were the nobles and owned most of the land and the cattle.

The Tutsi no longer control Rwanda, and in fact many have left the country. Tutsi now make up slightly less than 10 percent of the population. Most of them still live by raising cattle.

Hutu Eighty-eight percent of the people in Rwanda are Hutu. They are a stocky, muscular people, averaging about five feet, five inches tall. Little is known about their origins, except that they are a Bantu people who came from somewhere near the equator.

Traditionally the Hutu have been farmers, but they have also followed such trades as blacksmithing and beekeeping. Many Hutu are still farmers, though a number of them now have government jobs. With education becoming more easily accessible, more and more Hutu are gradually leaving their farms to train for other jobs.

Other peoples A small number of nomads still wander through northern and

This Tutsi man wears his hair in a typical way: a crescent of hair on each side of the head.

northeastern Rwanda. They are the Hima. As did the Tutsi, to whom they are often said to be related, the Hima originated somewhere around the Nile and are cattle keepers.

Legend says that Rwanda once belonged to the ancestors of the Hima. According to the old stories, they lost the land because of illness and evil deeds. Because of these old tales, some people regard the Hima as bringers of bad luck and will have nothing to do with them.

At present there are about fifteen thousand citizens of Zaïre living in Rwanda. They are settled mostly in the western border area. There are also about five thousand Europeans, who are missionaries, teachers, businessmen, and government advisers. About three thousand persons of Asian descent live in Rwanda. They are primarily small businessmen, though a number of them work for the government in clerical or technical positions.

CUSTOMS AND BELIEFS

Despite the historical differences between Hutu and Tutsi, they have much in common. A belief in the importance of cattle, an idea that originated with the Tutsi, is shared by the Hutu as well. Kinyarwanda, originally the language of the Hutu, has been spoken by every Rwandan for many centuries. Often it is not easy to tell from which people an idea or a custom first came, since almost all Rwandans share general ideas about religion and personal behavior.

About 40 percent of the people of Rwanda have become Christians. Most of these converts are Roman Catholics. Especially in the rural areas, Rwandan Christians often keep some of their old beliefs along with their new ones.

The Asians in Rwanda follow Islam, Hinduism, or Buddhism. These religions are most important in the cities, since that is where most of the Asians live.

The traditional religion, *animism,* is still the religion of most Rwandans. It is based on a belief in Imana, creator of the universe and source of all good. This religion teaches that all men and animals possess the same inner spirit, called *imana.* This living spirit is believed to be in everything—human beings, plants, stones, water, and fire. When animals die, their spirits vanish. When human beings die, their spirits are honored as ancestors and referred to as *bazimu.* There is a strong feeling that all things are in the hands of Imana. Men must try to lead good lives, but in the end everything depends on Imana. A Rwandan proverb says, "If Imana is walking elsewhere during the day, he will come home at night to Rwanda."

Rituals are also very important in the traditional religion. They must be performed by certain people, and usually take place during harvest time or at special occasions such as births or weddings. Special societies—often with secret memberships,

Young Tutsi girls. Today Rwandan children—both Tutsi and Hutu—share similar beliefs and ways of life.

but always with elaborate rituals—are dedicated to Ryangombe, the leader of a family of ancestral spirits, and to Nyabungi, a female ancestor.

Medicine is practiced by *curers,* people who use special rituals in their work. Curers, called *abafumu* (plural of *umufumu*) have many different specialties. Some of them cure ailments by preparing medicines from plants. Others supply amulets (charms believed to aid or protect the owner against evil) and perform rituals to ward off misfortunes caused by witches or angry ancestral spirits. Still others interpret dreams or predict the future. A group of abafumu, called *ababvubyi,* are rainmakers. They must be very careful, for if they fail to create rain, they can be punished by the person who asked for the rain.

65

Members of a Twa family make pottery in their compound.

THE FAMILY

Life in Rwanda revolves around the family. Most Rwandans do not live in towns or even in villages; instead, families live together in a fenced compound called a *rugo*.

The rugo is made up of houses grouped around the main family homestead. The land immediately surrounding the rugo is used as the family's farmland and grazing land. Family compounds are scattered across the countryside on hilltops.

Family ties are extremely strong—so strong that there are no unattached persons in Rwanda. Orphans are automatically taken in by members of their parents' families. They are raised as children of the household they join.

The father is the head of the Rwandan family. All family members obey him. In the past, in some very strict families, respect for the father was so strong that children were not even allowed to pronounce his name.

The most important social grouping in Rwanda is the *umuhara,* a group of people who are related to and live near each other. The umuhara brings its members together to perform religious ceremonies and to deal with government authorities.

BIRTH AND DEATH

Everyone is happy when a child is born, since a boy will keep the clan powerful

66

and a girl will bring a bridewealth. Children are usually born at home. The mother is helped by her neighbors and by the local midwife. When the baby is born, it is washed in cold water and rubbed with butter. After six days, relatives bring gifts to the mother and the baby.

The death rate among babies in the first three or four months of life is very high in underdeveloped areas throughout the world. In Rwanda, families wait until that danger period is over before naming their babies. The father selects the name. It is chosen according to how the father would like the child to grow up, and also according to such factors as events during the child's birth, well-known events, or characteristics of Imana. The baby is also given nicknames, since it is believed that harm may come to a person called by his real name.

When a person dies, his family stops all work. Relatives and neighbors bring food and firewood, and also do the family chores for several days or longer. Most of the people believe that spirits live on in the dead. The ancestral spirits have a small, special house of their own that is built as part of the family compound. The head of the house is buried within the compound—this is a place of honor. Other family members are buried nearby.

The period of mourning varies, depending on the status of the dead person. Traditionally, mourning for the mwami lasted as long as an entire year. During this time no giving of life was permitted. Because of this prohibition, no crops could be planted; often this resulted in starvation, along with a great deal of frustration among the people. Among most Rwandans, the mourning period lasts for two months.

WEDDINGS AND GIFTS

Fathers have much to say about choosing their sons' wives. Even if the sons choose for themselves, they must have the father's approval. The family must also pay the *bridewealth*, the payment given to the bride's parents. This is usually paid in cattle, goats, or hoes. A bridewealth can be expensive and a young man cannot usually pay it himself. Payment of the bridewealth makes a marriage proper and official. If the marriage breaks up, the bride's family must return the bridewealth. If there are children involved in a divorce, the father must pay to keep them. The people of Rwanda, however, feel that children belong to the father and his family, not to the mother. The mother, according to Rwandan custom, belongs to *her* father and his family—even though she is married.

Gifts are an important part of weddings and many other occasions. A marriage is not valid until the bride moves to the groom's compound and gifts have been exchanged.

Because there is a shortage of land in Rwanda, today newly married couples sometimes must move far away from the groom's family. Though many move to government-sponsored farm areas called *paysannats,* they try to visit their families frequently.

On the wedding day, or *bukwe,* the groom and his friends go to the bride's house, where they present the bridewealth to the parents. They also bring other gifts to console the bride for having to leave her family. It is traditional for the bride to cry when leaving her home, but soon she is led away. The actual wedding ceremony is called the *kurongora.* After this ceremony, which symbolizes the bride's future motherhood, the bride goes to the groom's home to meet his family. A festive party follows, but the bride's parents do not attend.

Both families give gifts to the new couple. Long after the wedding, the husband gives occasional gifts to his wife's family. When the bride's mother comes to see her daughter, she often brings a little gift. When a woman has a child, she and

the child are both given gifts. Business deals are sealed with an exchange of gifts.

Beer is a frequent gift, since it is a necessary part of all social occasions. It is always drunk at funerals or weddings. Any formal or informal visit, or even a chance meeting, is made special by offering a drink of beer. Beer drinking is a symbol of the people's hospitality toward each other.

Rwandans brew most of their beer at home. It is made from bananas, millet, sorghum, or honey. Often beer is served in a single, large clay pot. Each person drinks from it through his own straw, made from a reed.

To refuse beer can be a serious insult. This is because Rwandans always refuse to drink with a man who has done something to make others lose respect for him. People may say of someone who is behaving in an unpleasant manner, "If he goes on that way, no one will drink with him."

Nearly everyone in Rwanda marries when still young. Far left: Bride and groom with guests at a Hutu wedding. Left: A woman holds her child.

The People Work in Rwanda

Rwanda is a land of farmers; 93 percent of the people in Rwanda are supported by agriculture. Most crops are raised on small family farms and are eaten by the family that raises them.

A TYPICAL FARM

The entire compound, called the rugo, is made up of the main homestead and a number of other houses. The very small houses are for the ancestors, the medium-sized houses are for the sons, and the main house, which is the largest, is for the father.

The houses are built of thatch, and a clay solution made with cow dung serves as a wash to cover the thatching and insulate the houses. The cow dung makes the clay solution strong and supportive when it dries. These houses are in the traditional central African beehive shape. A fence, made by lashing many young trees and branches close together, surrounds the rugo. Sometimes the fence is given a wash like the one used to cover the houses.

The family lives in the rugo. Cattle are brought inside the rugo walls at night. Outside the walls is usually a grove of banana plants, as bananas are an important part of the family diet. The plants bear fruit all year.

A boy and a girl stand in the entrance to their compound.

Near the rugo is the plot of land on which the family raises its reserve food. The reserve crops are edible roots such as manioc and sweet potatoes, which can be stored easily for quite a long time. Though they are part of the daily diet, most reserve crops are stored and saved to guard against hunger in case hail or drought should ruin other crops. The farmer's fields are scattered to help prevent total crop destruction.

High upon a hillside, often a mile or more from the rugo, are the plots where the family's staple foods are grown. Peas, beans, corn, and sorghum, as well as millet and eleusine, the main cereals, are grown here. There is usually still another piece of family land in a low-lying area that is also planted with vegetables. The family depends on these vegetables during the dry season, the time when the growing season has ended in the drier, higher regions.

Finally, a last bit of land, often isolated from the others, is carefully chosen for the family's coffee trees. If the family has any cash income, it is from coffee, Rwanda's most important cash crop. Half of the money Rwandans receive for goods sold to other countries is earned by coffee alone.

The many hills and small family plots make tractors impractical in Rwanda. Even ox-drawn plows are difficult to use in many places. A heart-shaped hoe, used throughout central Africa, is one of the main farm tools. The other tool is the *serpette,* a small, sharp sickle attached to a handle; it looks like a pruning knife. Hutu craftsmen have long used the abundant, local iron ore to make other tools such as the axe and the *adaze*—a cutting tool whose thin, arched blade is perpendicular to the handle.

PROBLEMS AND SOLUTIONS

Many factors have brought perennial hunger to Rwanda: the subtropical climate, with six months of rain and six dry months; the high population density; and the great amount of land not suitable for growing crops. These problems are too big for farmers to tackle individually. Because they need everything they can grow, farmers are afraid to take chances on new methods. That is why the government of Rwanda is trying hard to find new solutions to these problems.

Agricultural experts say that a farm family today needs from five to twelve acres of land, depending on where they live. With that much land, a family could support itself and use the land properly, without exhausting it by overfarming.

A girl carrying a basket on her head passes by a banana plantation. Bananas are basic to the diet of most Rwandans.

A farmer puts out his coffee beans to dry. Because there is much sunshine throughout the year, coffee and other crops such as beans and maize can usually be left out to dry.

Rwanda is a crowded country. The average farm family in Rwanda today has even less than four acres; yet almost all the farmable land is being used. Only about 10 percent of land that could be farmed is not planted. This land is in eastern Rwanda, where lack of water is a problem.

The government has been concerned about the overcrowding of land since before independence. Areas that had very few people have been made into paysannats—farmlands to which people could move when the rugos became too crowded. Each paysannat is devoted to the growing of a particular crop. Coffee is grown on most of the paysannats, while pyrethrum, cotton, and tea are grown on the others. Most of the paysannats are located in the south-central part of the country.

The second great problem in Rwanda is soil erosion. Heavy rains wash the topsoil off the hillsides. Both lack of trees and intensive use of the soil for crops and cattle have contributed to soil erosion. The government is teaching farmers to rotate their crops—plant different crops every year on the same soil in order to fight erosion and increase the yield on their crops. Trees and hedges are being planted to hold the soil in place.

The government has tried to introduce new crops such as peanuts, rice, soybeans, and sugarcane to the farmers of Rwanda.

Peanuts have been raised for many years in Rwanda. The peanut crop was introduced by Europeans, though peanuts are not liked or used much by Rwandans. With Belgian aid, however, carefully planned peanut farms have been set up on some eastern land, and the crops are doing well.

Rice cultivation was begun a few years ago. With the help of Nationalist China, about seven hundred acres of marshes have been sown in rice. Soybeans have been introduced as the year's second crop on the same land. There have been good harvests of both crops, though the people have trouble cooking soybeans and do not like them very well.

Sugarcane is also being tried as a commercial crop, with help from Nationalist China. It is being rotated with rice and vegetables.

CASH CROPS

Coffee is the country's chief cash crop. Most of the coffee raised in Rwanda is of a kind called Arabica coffee. An average farmer has about one hundred coffee trees. Each tree yields only about one and one-half pounds of parchment coffee—that is, coffee not yet roasted.

More fertilizers and more careful cultivation will increase the yield of coffee from each tree. Government experts are teaching better farming methods to the farmers. Improved varieties of coffee trees have also been planted.

Tea is another important cash crop in Rwanda. In the future, it may become the most important one, since tea is a nearly ideal crop for the country. Much of Rwanda's land—forty-two thousand acres—is well suited to tea farming. It is fortunate that this land is swamp and marsh and otherwise difficult to use.

Compared to almost all the other crops that grow well in Rwanda, tea is relatively inexpensive to ship. A small shipment is quite valuable. That fact is important to a country located more than a thousand miles from the nearest seaport.

Unfortunately, tea is not a good crop for small farmers; it is better suited to large plantations. Preparing and planting fields of tea takes more work and money than most individual farmers can supply. Trained labor must care for the plants, and the crop must be processed quickly after its harvest.

Commercial tea cultivation was begun in Rwanda more than twenty years ago. Since then production has risen steadily, and now there are about a dozen large plantations. Since Rwanda could sell more tea than it now produces, the government is strongly encouraging increased plant-

Men cultivate rows of pyrethrum flowers in a field. Grown at high altitudes in volcanic soil, this flower is the base of a powerful insecticide and is an important export product.

ing. Some of the tea plantations are financed by Europeans, but two are on paysannats and aided by the government.

Pyrethrum is Rwanda's other main export crop. It is a small flower, very much like a daisy. Part of the pyrethrum is dried and used to make insecticides. Pyrethrum is grown at high altitudes in areas that receive large amounts of rain, but where no other cash crops could be grown. Some of the world's best pyrethrum is grown in Rwanda.

CATTLE

In Rwanda, as in many African countries, owning cattle has always been considered to be a sign of wealth. Cattle have also been an important food source in Rwanda for a long time, especially for milk. Since abolishing ubuhake (the traditional agreement between owner and user of the cattle), cattle seem to have been losing some of their importance as a display item.

At one time in Rwanda, cattle were thought of only as signs of wealth. Today many people own cattle and they have become an important food source, especially for milk.

Market is a bright, bustling, cheerful place. Above: Women sit in rows, spreading out their products on the ground in front of them. Right: People buy bananas from a man at his truck.

Though vaccination has controlled many animal diseases, half the cattle still have tania worm; thus they cannot be sold for human consumption as beef. From 25 to 35 percent of all calves die of East Coast fever, a disease carried by ticks. Nagana, a variety of sleeping sickness, is widespread. The government is presently trying to eliminate the tsetse fly, which carries nagana.

People are reluctant to sell their cattle in the marketplace. They prefer to keep the cattle in order to have the milk and butter for themselves. Because the soil has too much acid, the cow manure—usually an excellent fertilizer—cannot always be used. Hygiene is also a problem. Both the cattle and the people need better health care to prevent the spread of such diseases as tuberculosis and worms.

Another drawback to raising cattle is that the herds of Renga cattle, with their long, lyre-shaped horns, are very thin and not of great value for beef, milk, or butter. After the cattle have fed their calves, they produce no more than one or two quarts of milk daily. This is not enough to sell, but the people make a popular form of yogurt out of it.

Though only a small quantity of butter is produced, there is always a market for it. Especially during the dry season, butter is used as a skin cream, and is viewed as a cosmetic that may be mixed with local perfumed wood.

There are too many cattle for the amount of pastureland available. Cattle chew the grass too close to the ground. Because of this, they are undernourished and the soil is left unprotected against eroding rains. Somehow, the government must convince people to keep fewer cattle, since smaller, healthier herds would be better for the country.

INDUSTRY

Manufacturing is just beginning in Rwanda. It is difficult to create a market for industry in Rwanda since very few people have money to buy manufactured goods. Also, there is not enough skilled labor in Rwanda. When many unskilled workers must be used, prices go up. Food processing and textile factories will probably provide the best means of expanding Rwanda's industry. The country has large reserves of natural gas, which can be used to produce such products as fertilizers, explosives, plastics, and synthetic fabrics.

Most industry is located in the capital city of Kigali. Some shoes and clothing are made there and soft drinks are made in a modern plant. Various small plants produce soap, paints, and smallpox and rabies vaccines.

Several plants have been opened to assemble goods whose parts are manufactured abroad. Products such as radios, phonographs, and metal furniture can be shipped to Rwanda much more cheaply in parts than assembled; thus, they can be sold in Rwanda for less money.

Most of the industry in Rwanda is *cottage industry*—small articles are manu-

A woman weaves a basket out of raffia. Much of the cottage industry in Rwanda is produced in people's homes.

factured in people's homes or in nearby workshops. In Rwanda, cottage industry produces such articles as bricks, furniture, crates, pottery, and baskets.

MINING AND ENERGY

There are large amounts of various minerals in Rwanda. From 30 to 40 percent of the country's exports are minerals. Tin is the country's most important mineral export, followed by tungsten and beryl.

All of the clay, sand, gravel, lime, and building stone that are produced are used within Rwanda.

Even without any known coal or oil deposits, Rwanda has a good source of power in its many rivers and streams. Dams could turn their movement into electricity, thus producing vast amounts of power. Large deposits of methane gas are known to exist in the depths of Lake Kivu. The gas could supply power for factories and also be used to make fertilizers or other synthetic chemical products.

The sights of Rwanda are spectacular. Here people walk along an unpaved road, surrounded by giant trees.

Enchantment of Rwanda

THE SIGHTS

Many people have called Rwanda the most beautiful place in Africa: the hills and sparkling streams and lakes are magnificent. The climate is very agreeable—both because Rwanda's average altitude is almost one mile above sea level and because cool trade winds blow in from the Indian Ocean. The pleasantness of the climate makes it hard to believe that Rwanda is only a few miles south of the equator.

Though Rwanda's road system is rather extensive, it is generally poor; very few roads are paved. In spite of this, Rwanda's main attractions—the Kagera National Park and Lake Kivu—are still visited by more and more people each year.

Kagera National Park covers about one thousand square miles of land in eastern Rwanda, about 10 percent of the country's total land area. Separated from the park by a road is the Mutara Big Game Hunting Reserve. Hunting is permitted there under strict government controls. In the town of Gabiro, located on the Kigali-Kampala road, there is a hotel for people visiting these reserves.

Rwanda's western border is on part of Lake Kivu. On the shores of this lake grow beautiful, thick vegetation, including some banana plantations; there are also a number of beaches. The lake itself is at an altitude of 4,700 feet and its waters are cool and clear.

Located on Lake Kivu is the town of Gisenyi. It has a number of pleasant hotels, a beautiful beach, and a handsome, paved main street bordered by trees.

Near Gisenyi is Albert National Park, shared by Zaïre and Rwanda. Most of the

park is in Zaïre, but a section of it is in Rwanda's volcano region. This region, known as the Virunga Range, has five forest-covered volcanoes. The tallest volcano, called the Karisimbi, is 14,800 feet high. The Muhabura Volcano, 13,510 feet high, is the home of the few remaining gorillas in Rwanda.

Other interesting areas of Rwanda include the capital city of Kigali; the town of Butare (home of the National University of Rwanda); the forests of Nyungwe; and the Congo-Nile dividing crest, whose mountains rise to almost ten thousand feet. Seen from a distance these mountains are very beautiful. Because the mountains are so close to the equator, mist and sometimes snow give the scenery a very special and exciting appearance.

THE SOUNDS

Not only the scenery of Rwanda is attractive. A visitor who has time to stay awhile in the countryside finds that the sounds of the country are just as enchanting as its sights.

The sounds of Rwanda are musical ones. Music is likely to be heard at almost any moment. Everyone is Rwanda is involved in music in some way. While some are playing instruments, others join in by

On the shores of Lake Kivu are many banana plantations. Far left: Villagers load bananas into dugouts. Left: The beach at Kisenyi. This area has become a major tourist center.

singing, dancing, and clapping their hands. Of course, as in all other countries, there are professional musicians in Rwanda who specialize in making music.

Music used to be part of each day's life in Rwanda. Large and small occasions were accompanied by music. There were many work songs, as well as special songs for different activities. For example, some songs were sung when paddling a canoe *against* the current, while others were sung when paddling *with* the current.

The Hutu, Tutsi, and Twa each had their own distinctive songs. For example, the Twa had songs about hunting, their favorite occupation, as well as songs about war. The Hutu had a large number of songs for special occasions such as hunting, harvesting, and beer-drinking, and songs for praising a chief. Some Hutu songs from colonial days made fun of Tutsi lords and Belgian officials.

The Tutsi also had many songs with particular uses. There are songs to boast of their exploits as warriors, to praise cattle, to flatter a girl, to recall absent friends, and to greet a visitor. Quite naturally, many Tutsi songs were about cattle; there were songs to be sung when drawing water for the cattle, when taking the herd home in the evening, and when showing the cattle to a guest.

*The sounds of Rwanda are as enchanting as the sights.
Above: Bells tingle and feet stomp as dancers perform
at the Independence Day celebrations. Right: Herdsmen
dance in front of a royal hut to the rhythmic beat of drums.*

Travelers would tell the news by chanting songs around their hosts' fires, sometimes accompanying themselves on a stringed instrument.

Many types of songs were discouraged by the Belgian colonial government and Christian missionaries. Some people have attempted to discover and record these and other songs, but the songs have become almost totally lost or hardly used at all.

Many kinds of musical instruments are played in Africa. Traditionally, they were all handmade. The kind of instruments that were played depended on the materials available. When there were good woods and reeds, there were flutes, drums, and stringed instruments. When suitable materials were not available, singing was the main kind of music.

Two of the most popular and most typically African instruments in Rwanda are the *mbira* and the drum. The mbira was invented in Africa. It is a small instrument with curved, narrow metal strips attached to a board or box. The metal pieces are plucked with the thumb to make

This man wears the traditional hairdo and clothing. The ways of the modern world have not changed the lives of the people who live in the isolated hills.

music; thus the mbira is sometimes called the "thumb piano." Its tones are gentle and delicate. It is not at all unusual in Africa to meet a lone traveler walking along the road, keeping himself company by playing a mbira.

In Rwanda, as in the rest of Africa, the drum is the most widely used musical instrument. Traditionally, it has been used for both music and for sending messages, though now it is used primarily for music. In Rwanda the drum is especially popular among the Tutsi. The Royal Drummers of the former mwami's court were famous throughout the world.

When Rwanda was a kingdom, a sacred drum called the karinga was the symbol of the mwami's power. It was used mostly for ceremonial occasions, including the very formal ritual dances of the Tutsi in celebrations involving the mwami. The karinga had the same importance in Rwanda as did the throne or crown in a European kingdom. The karinga was kept carefully wrapped in mats, since it was forbidden for the public to see it. It was brought out only on very special occasions. When the Hutu began their struggle against Tutsi control, the tradition of the karinga was one of the first things they wanted removed.

Drum playing is no longer a special Tutsi activity in Rwanda, but drums are still the favorite musical instrument. They are often played in a group, and an all-drum band may have from seven to nine drums. Different drums make different sounds ranging from low to high. Usually the basic rhythm is set by the soprano drum, the one with the highest tone. Often the leader of the orchestra plays the soprano drum.

Drums often provide the music for dancing. African dancing is very complex and stylized. Specialists who study it can help foreigners understand it by helping them hear all of what is happening. A drum orchestra may be playing in three or even four main rhythms. A visitor from Europe or America is used to hearing one main rhythm at a time, and to him the music may be very confusing. Also, African music is not based on the same scale as Western music is; so it often sounds quite strange to visitors.

AN ISOLATED COUNTRY

Rwanda is a small country in an isolated part of Africa. It is a charming, hilly place—in some ways quite characteristic of Africa and in some ways quite different. The way of life in Rwanda has undergone great changes since the coming of Europeans, and it still continues to change.

Rwanda's people have long been organized into a single society. Because of this, Rwanda does not face the problems of unifying the people into one nation—a problem faced by so many new African nations. Rwanda, however, does need to develop her resources and population, and is taking every available opportunity to move in that direction.

Handy Reference Section

INSTANT FACTS

Political:
Official Name—La République du Rwanda
Capital—Kigali
Monetary Unit—Rwandan franc
Official Language—Kinyarwanda and French
Religions—Traditional; Roman Catholic
Form of Government—Republic
Flag—Three vertical stripes (red, yellow, and green) with a large, black "R" in the center of the yellow stripe.

Geographical:
Area—10,186 square miles
Greatest Length (north to south)—110 miles
Greatest Width (east to west)—145 miles
Highest Point—14,800 feet
Lowest Point—2,700 feet

POPULATION

Total Population—3,800,000
Population of Capital—20,000
Population Density—373 persons per square mile
Population Growth Rate—3.2 percent

Population Distribution (by ethnic group):

Hutu	88 percent
Tutsi	10 percent
Twa	1 percent
Others	1 percent

PREFECTURES

Butare	Gitarama
Byumba	Kibungo
Cyangugu	Kibuye
Gikongoro	Kigali
Gisenyi	Ruhengeri

HOLIDAYS

January 1—New Year's Day
January 28—Democracy Day (abolition of the monarchy)
March 12—Feast of Patron Saint of the President of the Republic
May 1—Labor Day
July 1—Independence Day
September 25—Government Day
November 1—All Saints' Day
December 25—Christmas

?—Twa come to Rwanda

c. 1400—Hutu kingdoms long established in Rwanda; Tutsi arrive in Rwanda

1855—Burton and Speke come near Rwanda

1861—Speke reaches edge of Rwanda

1876—Stanley reaches edge of Rwanda

1885—Berlin Conference designates Rwanda a German "sphere of influence"

1894—Von Goetzen, first European explorer, arrives in Rwanda

1900—Missionaries begin work in Rwanda

1910—Belgium, England, and Germany agree on Rwanda's borders

1913—Coffee growing introduced

1916—Belgians occupy Rwanda

1923—Rwanda becomes mandated territory of the League of Nations

1925—Belgium combines administration of Ruanda-Urundi with that of Belgian Congo

1928-29—Famine

1929—Secondary school founded in Butare

1943—Native advisory councils established

1946—Rwanda becomes United Nations trust territory

1952—Ten-Year Development Plan initiated

1954—High Council of Rwanda ends ubuhake

1956—Adult males receive right to vote

1957—High Council of Rwanda calls for quick preparation for independence; APROSOMA and Hutu Social Movement are founded by Hutu

1959—APROSOMA becomes a political party; UNAR formed by Tutsi, September; Hutu Social Movement becomes PARMEHUTU; conflict between Hutu and Tutsi

1961—Hutu win elections for Legislative Assembly, October; 80 percent vote to abolish monarchy October; monarchy abolished; Grégoire Kayibanda elected president of republic

1962—Independence, July 1; Rwanda joins United Nations

1963—Rwanda becomes founding member of Organization of African Unity; National University of Rwanda established; tea growing introduced

1965—Grégoire Kayibanda reelected president of republic; national broadcasting system established

1967—Election law gives vote to all Rwandans eighteen and older

1969—Grégoire Kayibanda reelected with more than 90 percent of the vote

Index